EP Ancient History Printables:
Levels 1-4

This book belongs to:

_____

This book was made for your convenience. It is available for printing from the Easy Peasy All-in-One Homeschool website. It contains all of the printables from Easy Peasy's ancient history course for levels 1-4. The instructions for each page are found in the online course.

Easy Peasy All-in-One Homeschool is a free online homeschool curriculum providing high quality education for children around the globe. It provides complete courses for preschool through high school graduation. For EP's curriculum visit allinonehomeschool.com.

EP Ancient History Printables: Levels 1-4

ISBN: 9781080437436

First Edition: July 2019

Pyramid

Cut on solid lines.

Fold on dotted lines.

Glue or tape the tabs to the square bottom/base section.

You can leave this section unattached so you can open the pyramid and put lapbook pieces (or treasures!) inside!

Timeline Order

Cut out these timeline events and put them in order. Remember, in BC the bigger the number, the farther back in time you are.

551 BC Confucius is born	509 BC Roman Republic established
500 BC Adena mounds are built in Ohio	206 BC Han Dynasty begins in China
221 BC Shi Huangdi becomes first emperor of China	27 BC Octavian becomes ruler of the Roman Empire
44 BC Julius Caesar is killed	100 AD Paper invented in China
476 AD Roman Empire falls	500 AD Height of Mayan civilization
570 AD Muhammad is born	600 AD Islam spreads to North Africa
800 AD Arab traders brought paper from China	960 AD Song Dynasty founded in China
1215 AD English Magna Carta signed	2700 BC The Old Kingdom began in Egypt

Egyptian Hierarchy

Read about Egyptian workers and look at the chart about Egyptian society. Fill in your own chart. You can write the words or cut out the pieces at the bottom of the page

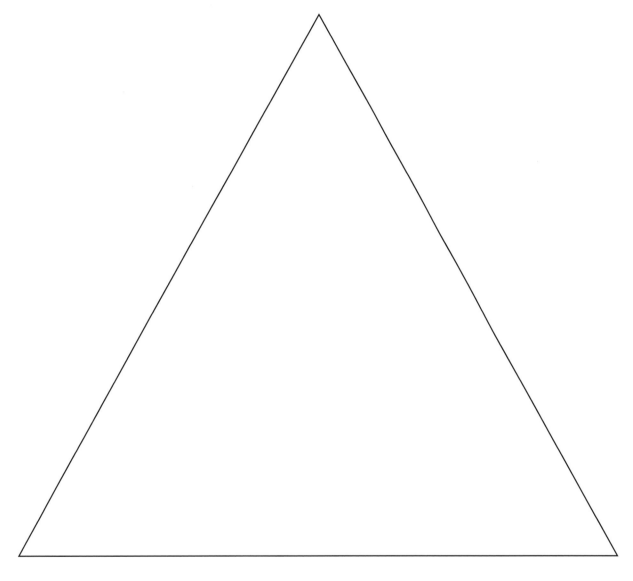

Priests	Craftsmen	Vizier (religious advisor)
Nobles	Pharaoh	Soldiers
Slaves	Scribes	Farmers

Hieroglyphic Code Break

Crack the code!

A	B	C	D	E	F	G	H	I	J
✌	👌	👍	👎	👉	☞	👆	☝	🖐	☺
K	**L**	**M**	**N**	**O**	**P**	**Q**	**R**	**S**	**T**
😐	☹	💣	☠	⚐	⚑	✈	☼	💧	❄
		U	**V**	**W**	**X**	**Y**	**Z**		
		✝	✞	☥	✠	✡	☾		

_____   _____

_____   _____   _____   _____

_____   _____   _____   _____

_____   _____   _____

_____

Rosetta Stone

The Rosetta stone was found in

_____. It was found by

French soldiers. The Rosetta stone

had writing carved on it. The same

order, or proclamation, was written

in three _____. They are:

an ancient Egyptian script called

Demotic, Ancient Greek, and

_____. This helped

people learn how to read

hieroglyphics and the ancient

Egyptian Demotic script.

Jean François Champollion studied

the Rosetta Stone and deciphered

the hieroglyphs. He read the

_____ writing and was able to

make educated guesses about the

meaning of the hieroglyphs.

Through a lot of study and work, he

was able to decipher the

hieroglyphic and Demotic writing

systems.

Word Bank:
GREEK
SCRIPTS
HIEROGLYPHICS
EGYPT

Papyrus

The ancient Egyptians made a form of paper called papyrus. Draw a picture in the box to match the directions for making papyrus.

Gather a large amount of river reeds. Cut off the outside layer of the reed. You may need to further cut the inside portion of the reeds into thinner strips.	
Weave the inside portions of the reeds like you are making a placemat.	
Pound the mat area to flatten it. You can use a rock, hammer, or rolling pin. This also helps remove water from the reeds. Make sure you flip it over and pound the other side as well.	
Leave your papyrus to dry. You can hang it in the sun to let it dry faster. When it is completely dry, you can write or draw on it!	

Embalming the Pharaoh

When the Pharaoh died, the body was prepared for burial. The embalming process required certain organs to be removed and placed into jars. Label each jar with the organ it contains. Mark off the labels to find out which organs were NOT placed into jars.

BRAIN   STOMACH   LIVER
INTESTINES   HEART   LUNGS

King Tut

Write something about what you have learned about King Tut.

_____

_____

_____

_____

_____

Draw a picture of one of the
treasures found in his tomb.

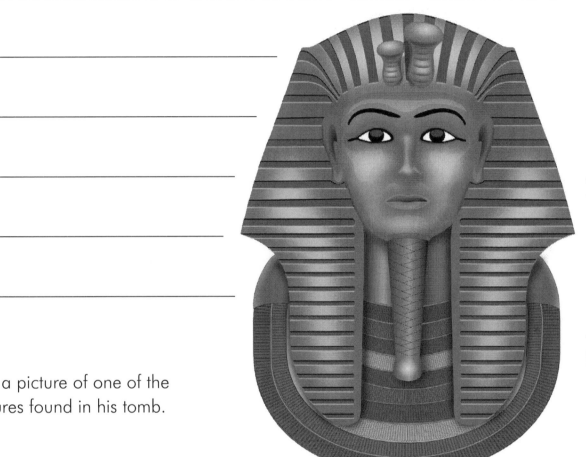

Word Find

Read these facts about ancient Egypt. Find the words in bold in the word search.

H	F	O	N	M	V	P
I	K	L	B	O	A	T
E	N	I	L	E	L	U
R	I	A	B	G	L	T
O	G	D	S	Y	E	L
G	I	Z	A	P	Y	B
L	Z	A	P	T	K	G
Y	T	U	B	E	W	I
P	O	T	T	E	R	Y
H	P	K	L	A	T	Q
I	K	P	M	A	S	K
C	L	W	A	N	O	Y
S	P	H	I	N	X	D

Life in ancient Egypt was centered around the **Nile** River. The main form of transport in ancient Egypt was the **boat**. Early Egyptians used clay to make **pottery**.

The ancient Egyptians developed a writing system called **hieroglyphics**.

The Great **Sphinx** and the Great Pyramid at **Giza** were built during the "Old Kingdom" period.

King **Tut** was a pharaoh that was buried in the **Valley** of the Kings with a beautiful gold **mask**.

King Tut

Color the picture of King Tut.

Ancient Egypt Timeline

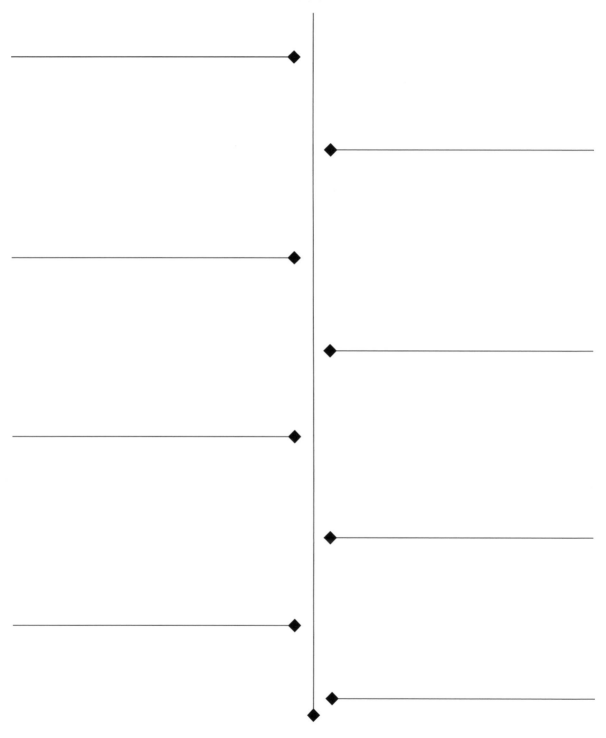

Mesopotamia

Color in the area known as Mesopotamia.

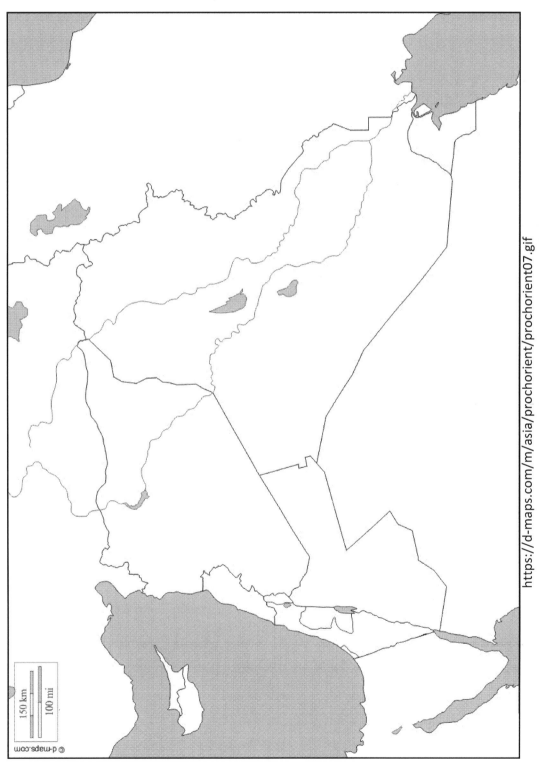

150 km

100 mi

© d-maps.com

Mesopotamia Timeline

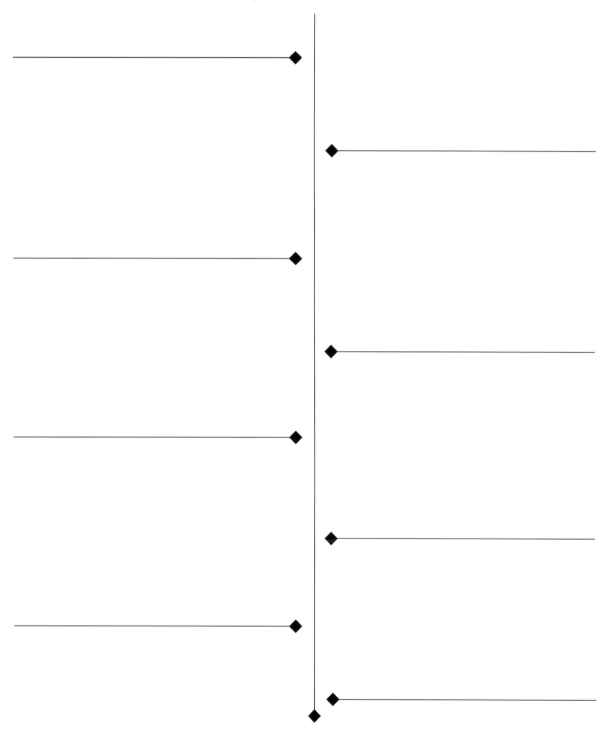

Current Events

Answer each question about the article you read.

What happened?

Who was there?

When did it happen?

Where did it happen?

Why did it happen?

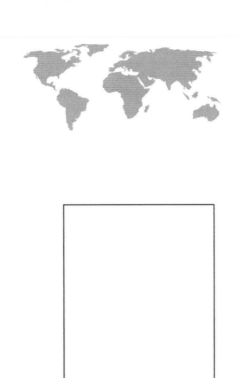

Cut out as two strips and attach together using the dark rectangle. This is your BC strip. Attach BC timeline pieces in order. Fold accordion style and write B.C. on the cover.

Cut out the two rectangle strips and attach together. Make these the AD timeline. Attach the timeline pieces in order. Fold accordion style. Write A.D. on the cover.

Cut out each rectangle and glue the pieces onto the timeline in chronological order. Remember that BC works backwards, the bigger the number the longer ago it was. The BC all go on one timeline. The AD all go on the other. There are more picture/date cards on the next page.

Compass
200 BC

Crossbow
500 BC

Toilet Paper
589 AD

Growing Rice
4000 BC

Rotary Fan
200 BC

Silk Making
3000 BC

Fork
2400BC

Tea
2000 BC

Salt
Making
2000BC

Matches
577 AD

Toothbrush
1490 AD

Paper Money
700 AD

Fireworks
960 AD

Printing
618 AD

Deck
of
Cards
700 AD

Exploding
Cannonball
1400 AD

Cut out each piece separately and attach
in chronological order to the timeline.

Confucius

Read and copy this quote from Confucius.

Teaching from Confucius

What you do not want done to you,

do not do to others.

_____

_____

_____

_____

Emperor Qin

Cut around this as one long rectangle, including the picture. Fold in the middle. This part gets glued down.

Part of the

Easy Peasy All-in-One Homeschool

Terracotta Warriors

Cut around the whole thing as one big rectangle, and fold down the middle. The blank rectangle gets glued down and the picture becomes the cover. Write on the inside to tell about the Terracotta Warriors.

Great Wall of China

Cut out each box with its tabs. Don't cut off the tabs!

1

How long is The Great Wall of China?

A   1,000 miles

B   4,000 miles

C   10,000 miles

2

When did the Chinese start to build the wall?

A   771 BC

B   45 BC

C   543 AD

3

Why did they build The Great Wall?

A   To decorate their country
B   To show off their abilities
C   To protect themselves

Continued on the next page.

Great Wall of China

Cut out the Great Wall box. Cut out the box with the 4 tab (don't cut off the tab!) Cut out the box with the "answers" tab. Stack all boxes with the picture on top, then in order 1, 2, 3, 4, answers.

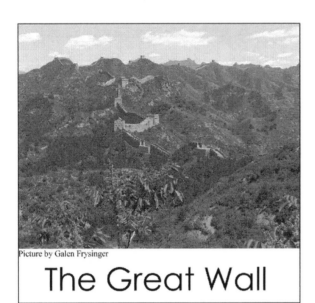

Picture by Galen Frysinger

The Great Wall

1 B, 4000 miles	You can see the Great Wall from outer space.
2 A, 771 BC	
3 C, To protect themselves	True or False
4 Not really. You can't see it from space without help.	4

Answers

Confucius

Copy the Confucius quote.

A man who has committed a mistake and doesn't correct it is committing another mistake.

Confucius

Copy the Confucius quote.

Consideration for others is the basis of a good society.

_____

_____

_____

_____

Tangrams

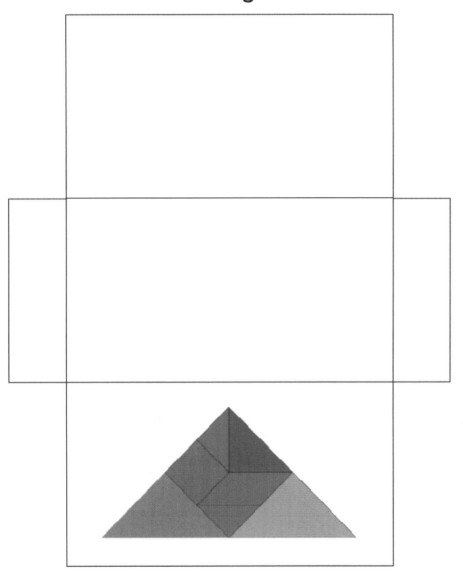

The first book mentioning **tangrams** was printed in China in 1813, but many believe the design is ancient.

Cut out word box separately. The rest cut out as one piece. Fold the top rectangle forward. Fold side flaps around that flap and attach to make pocket. (So the flaps are on the same side of the paper as the picture.) Fold down tangram picture flap to make the cover. (Now the little side flaps are on the back and the picture is on the front.) Lift the flap and attach the word box inside.

Cut out the tangram pieces along the lines. You will have 7 shape pieces when you are done. Put in the pocket made on the previous page. Use them to make different shapes and designs. There are patterns for the shapes to make at http://etc.usf.edu/clipart/galleries/math/tangram_solid_puzzles.php

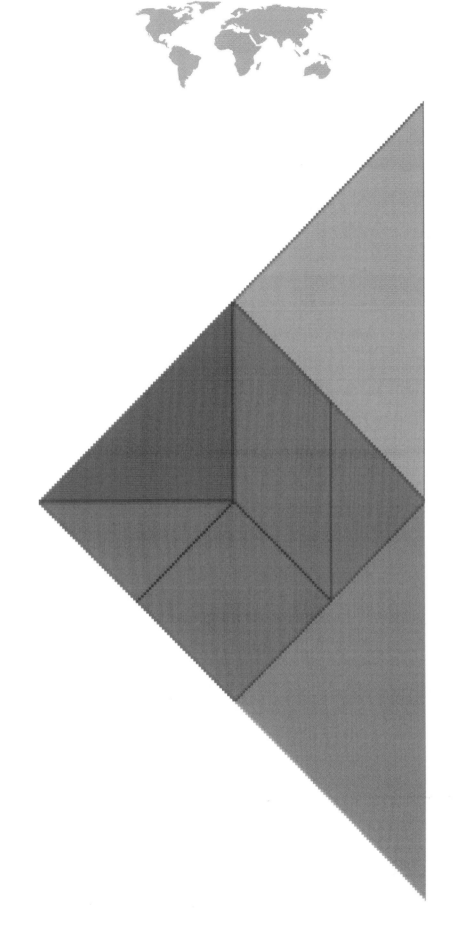

Silk Road

Write information you learned about the Silk Road. You can cut this out and use it as a lapbook piece or just use this page as a notebooking page.

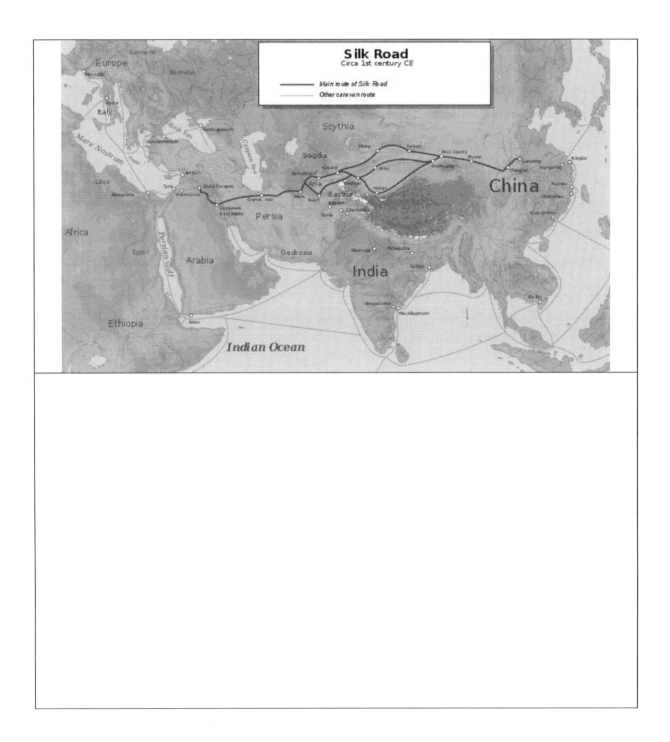

Indus Valley

Use this page to write notes about what you have learned about the Indus Valley Civilization.

Why did early civilizations begin around rivers? What were some of the important uses of water?

_____

_____

_____

Label the Indus River and color it blue. Look back at the map in your reading. Shade the Indus Valley civilization area.

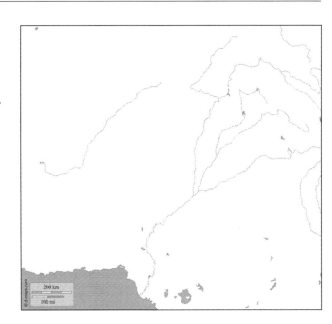

Look at the pictures from your reading assignment. Use this space to record your observations of the archaeologists' finds from the Indus Valley civilizations.

_____

_____

_____

Indus Valley

Cut out the pieces of this tabbed booklet. Stack all the pieces together and staple together at the bottom of the booklet.

My discoveries about the ancient cities of the Indus Valley

Why was the river important to the civilizations?

Cover page, Lesson 42

Daily life

Trade/Travel

Art/Writing

Page 2, Lesson 43

Jobs, Food

and Farming

Page 3, Lesson 44

Games/Toys

Page 4, Lesson 45

What they did
for us

Page 5, Lesson 46

Map Activity

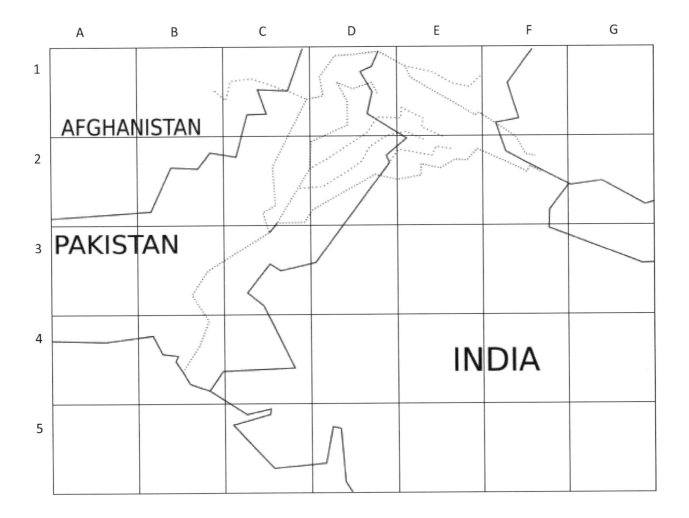

Color the dotted lines blue. Do you remember the name of the river? Label the river on the map.

Highlands are found in Pakistan, west of the Indus River. Color that area brown and label it "Highlands."

Draw a symbol to represent mountains in squares C1, D1, E1, F1, F2, and G2. Label the mountain range "Himalaya Mountains."

One major excavation site is Mohenjo-Daro. It is east of the Indus River in square B3. Mark and label that area on the map.

Another major area is Harappa. On your map, it is in square D2 between the lower 2 segments of the river system. Mark and label that area.

Fill in the Blanks

Fill in the blanks using words from the word bank.

Picture 1 shows an area excavated in Dholarvira. That is a reservoir that would have been full of _____ during the Indus Valley Civilization.

Picture 2 shows a _____. These were baked and cut to use in building the structures in the towns.

The clay sculptures in picture 3 were likely used as _____.

Picture 4 shows where a washroom would have been. The narrow, brick-lined area would have been a _____ taking dirty water away from the washroom.

The _____ and weights in picture 5 would have been used in trade and sales.

The seal in picture 6 has writing, an inscription of a deity with 3 faces, and several animals. The striped animal on the right is likely a _____.

Word Bank		
TIGER	WATER	DRAIN
TOYS	BRICK	SCALE

Current Events

What happened?

Who was there?

When did it happen?

Where did it happen?

Why did it happen?

Greece

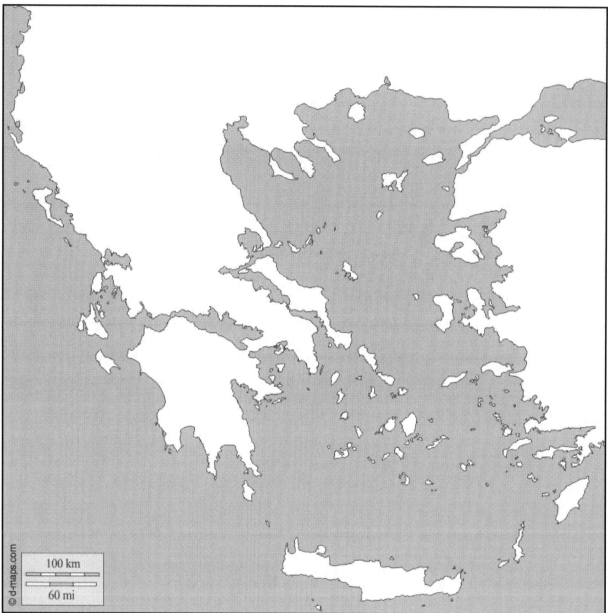

Choose a color to represent Greece.

Choose a symbol to represent Athens and Sparta.

Mark these places on the map.

Label the major bodies of water on the map.

Map Key	
	Greece
☺	Athens
⚑	Sparta

Map Source: https://d-maps.com/m/history/greceold/greceold01.gif

Trojan Horse

Write about the story of the Trojan Horse.

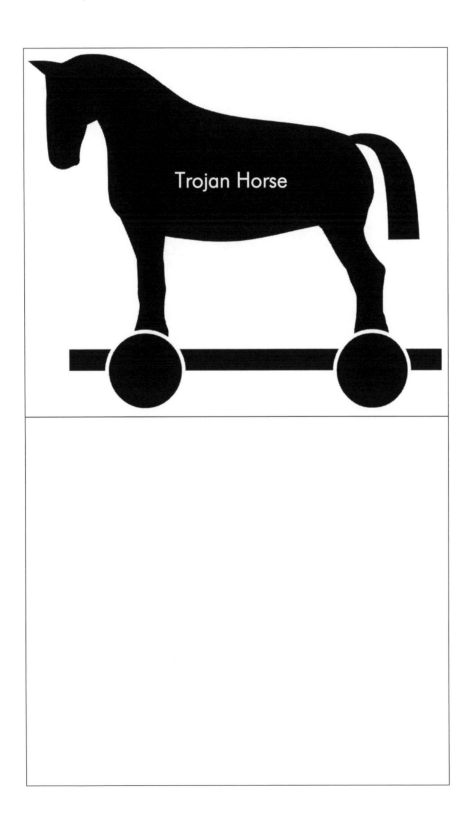

The Odyssey

The Odyssey
by Homer

Ancient Greece

Cut on the solid lines. Fold on the dotted lines to make a booklet. Write information about life in Ancient Greece.

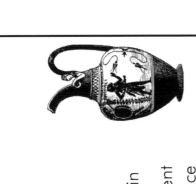

Life in
Ancient
Greece

Coloring Page

Choose one of the Greek gods you read about and color a design on the pottery to tell about him or her.

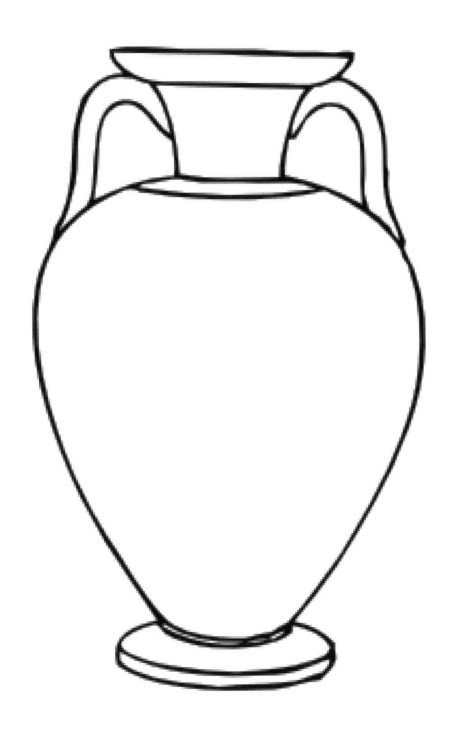

Parthenon

Fill in the blanks with words from the WORD BANK to complete the sentences.
Share with someone what you have learned about the Parthenon.

WORD BANK
sixty
columns
Athena
temple

The Parthenon was
built as a

_____ for worshipping the Greek gods.

Inside the Parthenon, there is a statue of _____.

The Parthenon is _____ feet tall.

The Parthenon has _____ on all sides.
Eight across the front and back and 17 along both of the other sides.

Sparta and Athens

Compare and contrast Sparta and Athens.

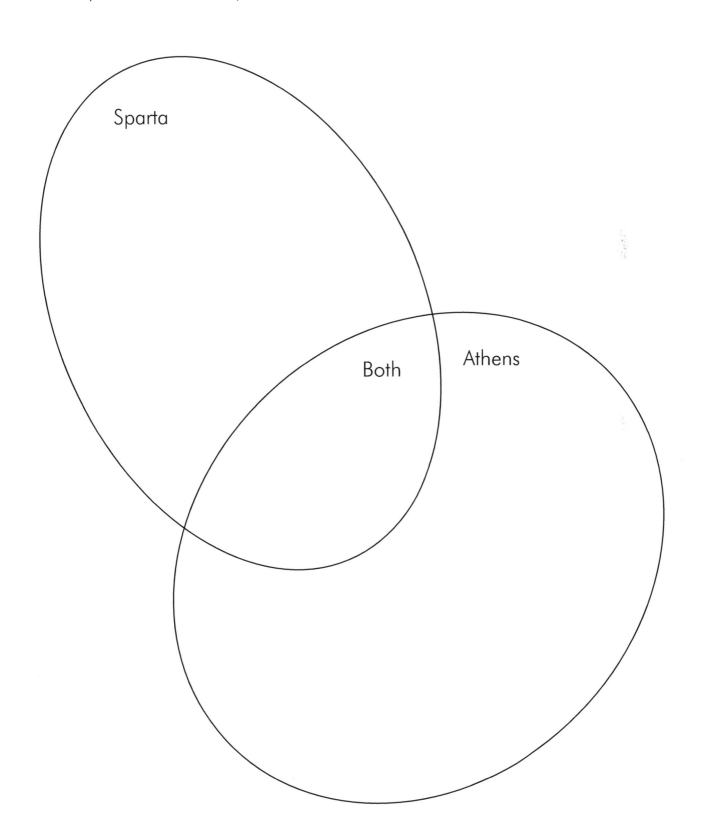

Sparta

Both

Athens

Matching

Match the Olympic event with the correct description.

Wrestling

Pentathalon

Boxing

Long jump

Horse racing

Javelin

Discus

This event consisted of five competitions: long jump, discus, javelin, running, and wrestling.

Some of these events took place on horseback. Others took place on chariots pulled by two or four horses.

This event was throwing a wooden spear.

This event was throwing an item shaped similar to a Frisbee.

This event took place in the sand. The match was over when a contestant was taken down three times.

Competitors would hold weights, swing them, then jump in a sand track.

Competitors were not allowed to hit below the belt.   Hitting in the head was allowed.

Ancient Greek Columns

Read the descriptions and write the name under the correct image.

DORIC – plain tops, not very decorative

IONIC – a little more decorative than Doric, basic column with a scroll design added

CORINTHIAN – fancier column with leaves

Draw your own Greek building. Which columns would you use?

Ancient Greek City-States

Use this graphic organizer to record what you learned about the ancient Greek city-states.

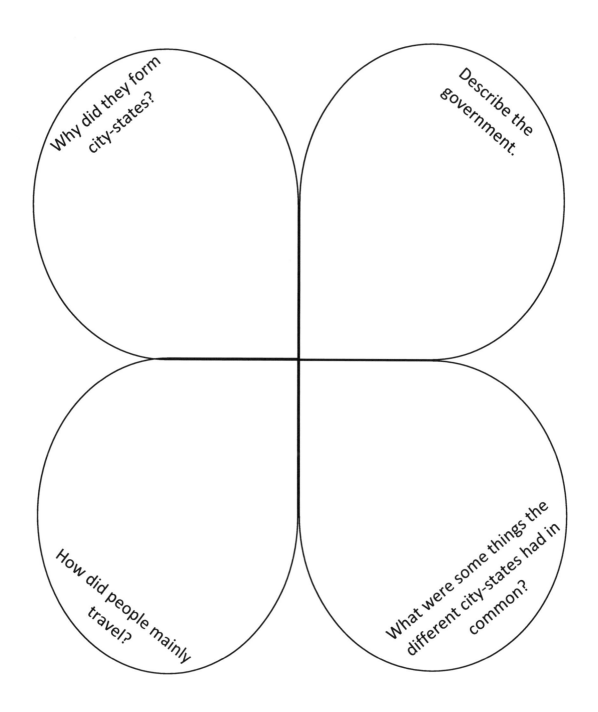

Why did they form city-states?

Describe the government.

How did people mainly travel?

What were some things the different city-states had in common?

Famous Greeks

Write information you learned about these famous Greeks. You can leave this as a worksheet or you could cut it out and use it as a lapbook piece.

Famous Greeks

Socrates

Hippocrates

Sophocles

Ancient Greek Theatre

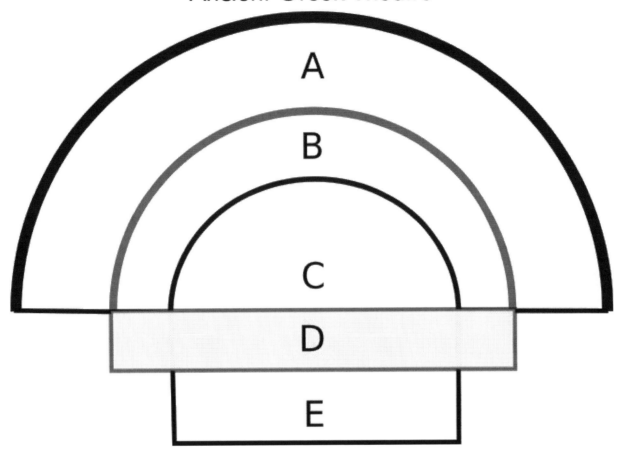

Match the letter to the area being described.

1. The two outer curved areas were seating areas. _____ and _____
2. The higher/outer seating area was for ordinary citizens. _____
3. The lower/inner seating area was for priests. _____
4. From the seating area, you can see the skene behind the stage. The skene was where actors would change or get ready. _____
5. Between the stage and the seating area was the orchestra area. The chorus would be in this area so they could be a part of the play and interact with the audience. _____
6. The stage was between the orchestra and the skene. Often it would be a simple wooden platform. _____

Current Events

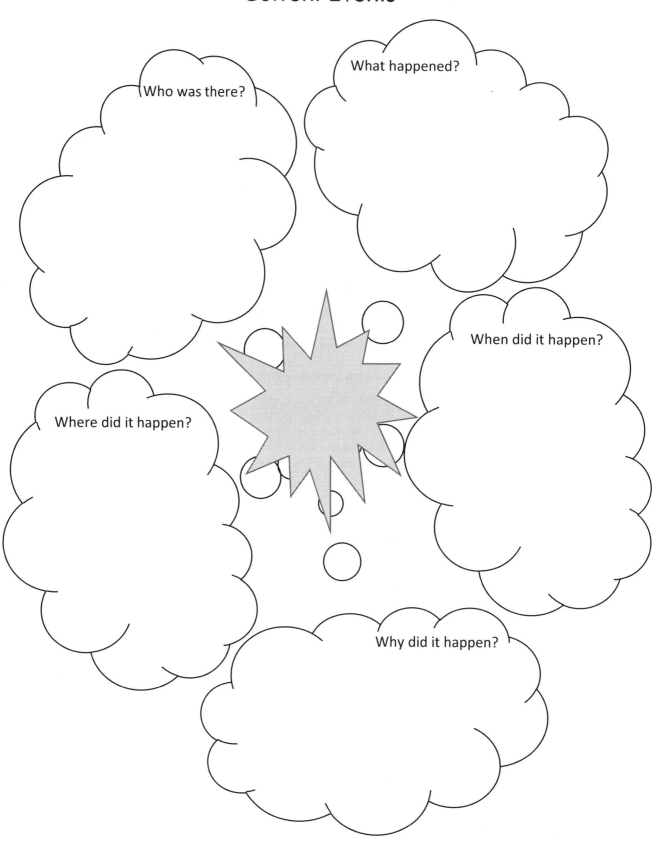

Who was there?

What happened?

When did it happen?

Where did it happen?

Why did it happen?

Current Events

What happened?

When did it happen?

Where did it happen?

Who was there?

Why did it happen?

Viking ships

Color these Viking ships.

Knights and Castles

Record what you have learned. You can leave this as a worksheet or cut it out to be a lapbook.

Castles:

Knights and Pages:

Coat of Arms

Japan

Find Japan on the top map and color it. Label the maps with the locations listed.

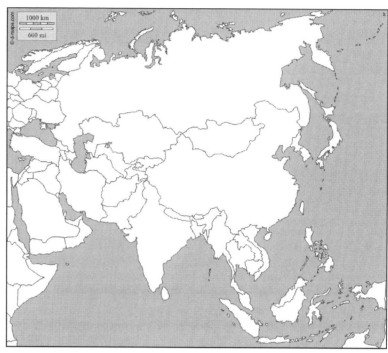

North Korea

South Korea

China

Sea of Japan

Pacific Ocean

Mount Fuji

Hokkaido

Honshu

Shikoku

Kyushu

Japan

Add notes to each class of the Japanese Feudal System.

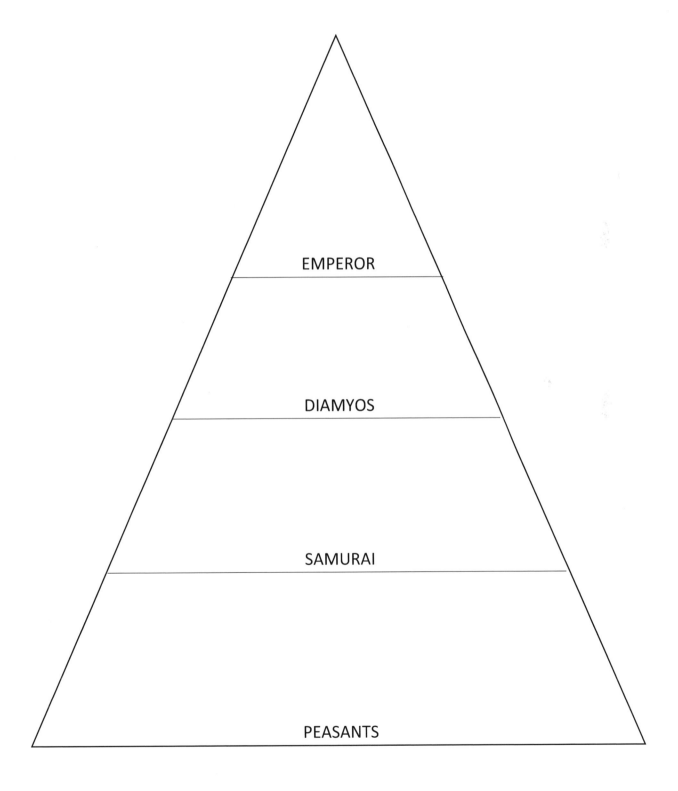

EMPEROR

DIAMYOS

SAMURAI

PEASANTS

Samurai

Samurai

Who were
they?

List some
of their
weapons.

What was
the code
of
bushido?

Japan: Kimono and Fan Dance

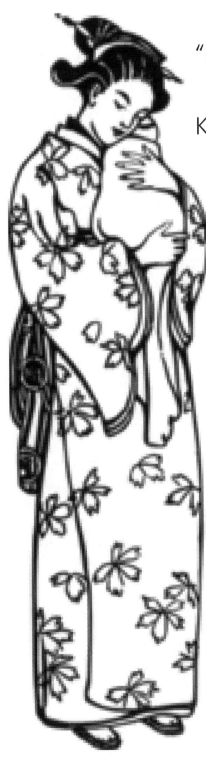

"Kimono" originally meant "something you wear."

Kimonos are long robes shaped like a "T" and usually covered in colorful designs.

Color the picture of the kimono.

Draw a picture below of the fan you would design for the traditional Japanese fan dance.

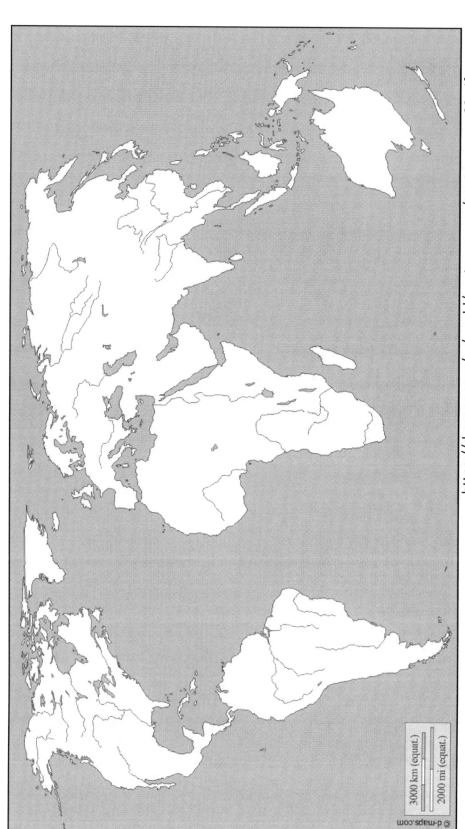

Mongol Empire

3000 km (equat.)

2000 mi (equat.)

@ d-maps.com

Current Events

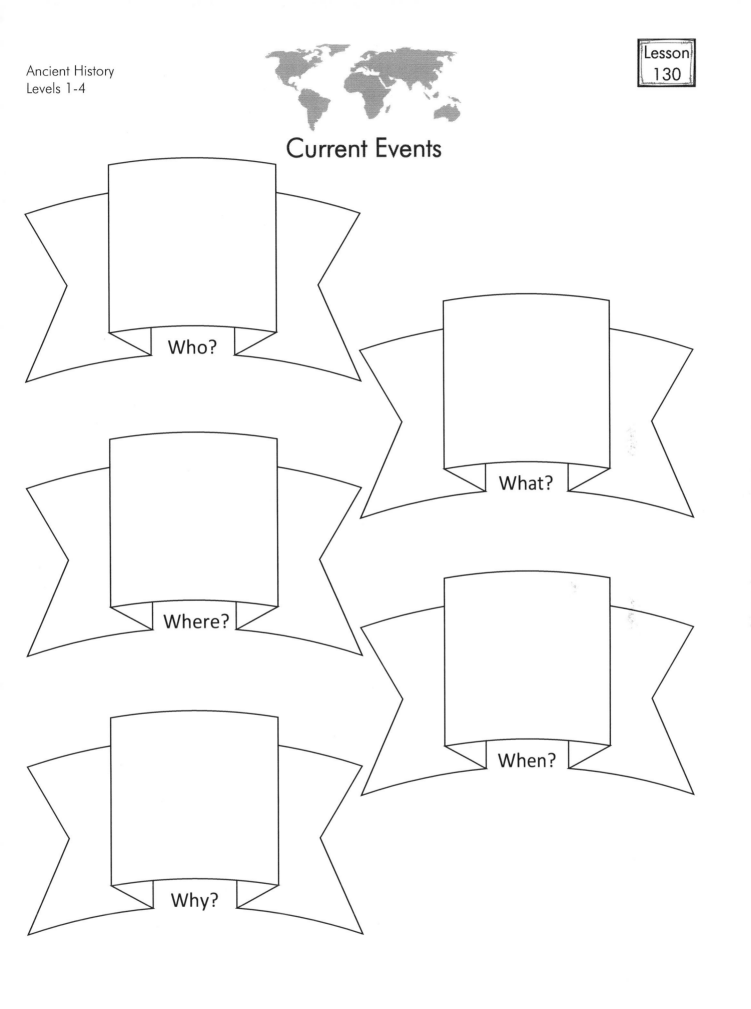

Who?

What?

Where?

When?

Why?

Ottoman Empire

Color the area showing where the Ottoman Empire ruled. Label Africa, Asia, and Europe.

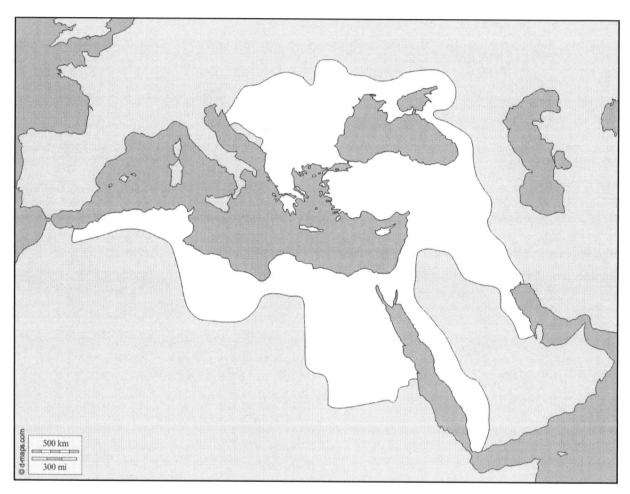

https://d-maps.com/m/history/ottomans/ottomans03.gif

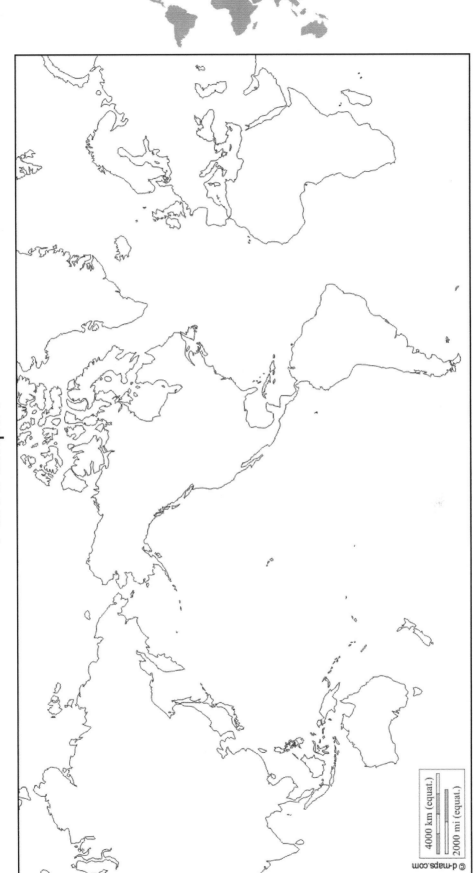

Aztec Empire

4000 km (equat.)

2000 mi (equat.)

© d-maps.com

Aztec Empire

Use the timeline available online to fill in information on this timeline.

Add information or events you found interesting on the blank lines.

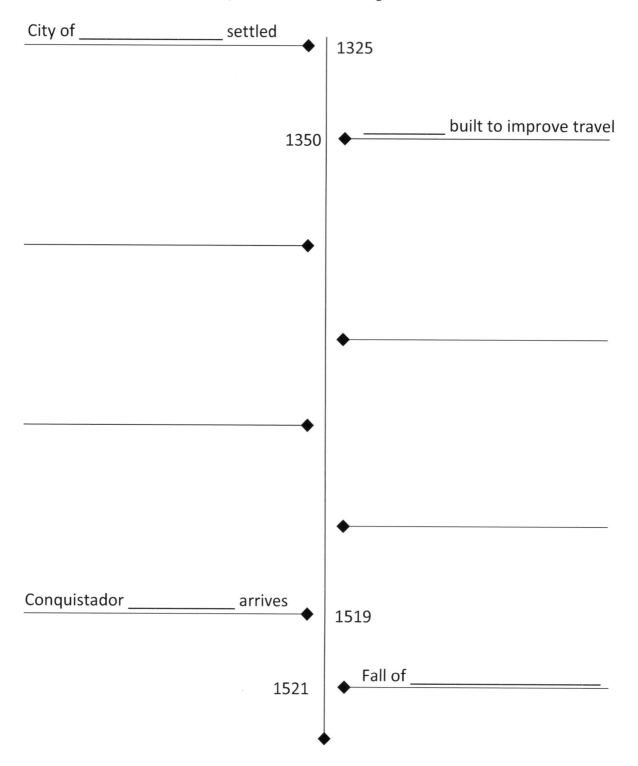

City of _____ settled ◆ 1325

1350 ◆ _____ built to improve travel

Conquistador _____ arrives ◆ 1519

1521 ◆ Fall of _____

Italy

Label Florence, Rome and Venice as closely as you can. Also label the
Mediterranean Sea.

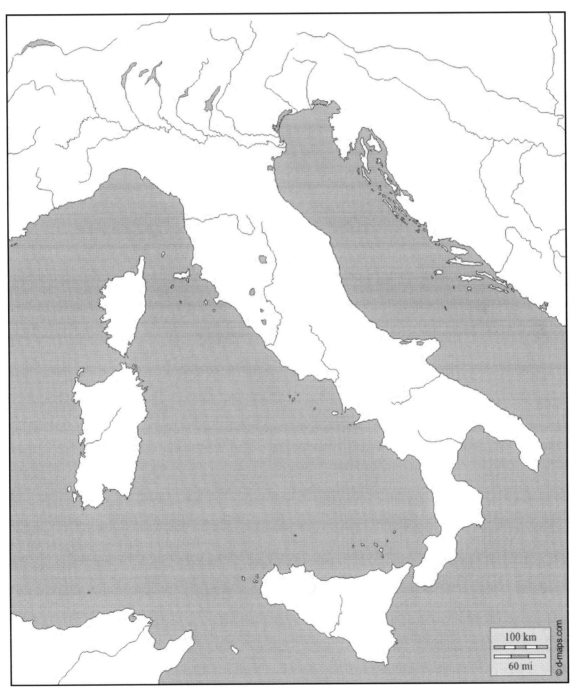

Choose a color to use to draw the route for each explorer.

☐ Magellan

☐ Drake

☐ Marco Polo

☐ Verrazano

☐ De Champlain

☐ Cabot

☐ Vasco Da Gama

☐ Ponce de Leon

☐ De Soto

☐ Hudson

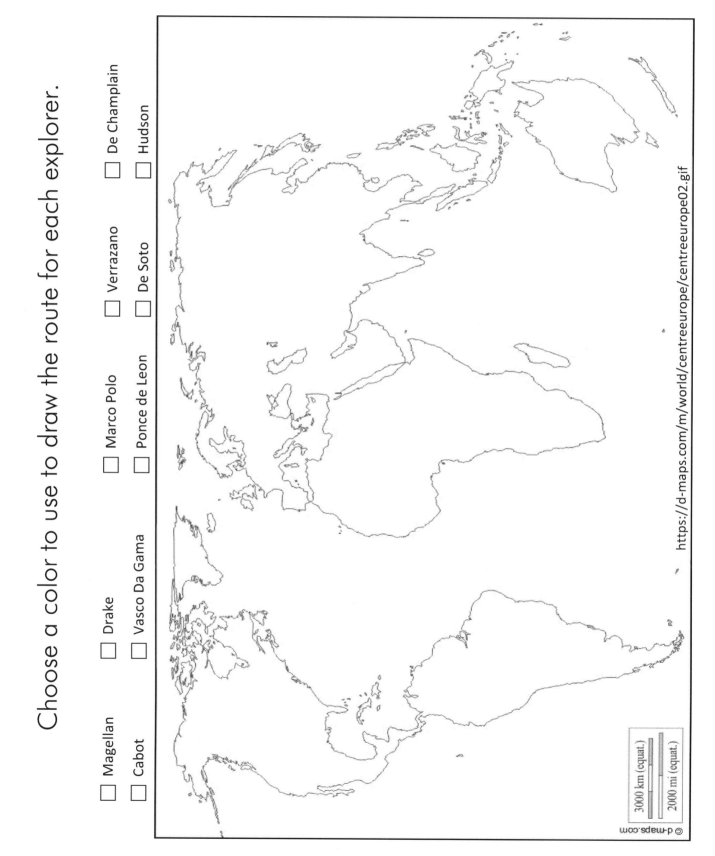

3000 km (equat.)

2000 mi (equat.)

© d-maps.com

https://d-maps.com/m/world/centreeurope/centreeurope02.gif

Research Report Note Taker

Topic: _____

Resource 1: _____

Info: _____   Info: _____

Info: _____   Info: _____

Info: _____   Info: _____

Resource 2: _____

Info: _____   Info: _____

Info: _____   Info: _____

Info: _____   Info: _____

Resource 3: _____

Info: _____   Info: _____

Info: _____   Info: _____

Info: _____   Info: _____

Resource 4: _____

Info: _____   Info: _____

Info: _____   Info: _____

Info: _____   Info: _____

Resource 5: _____

Info: _____   Info: _____

Info: _____   Info: _____

Info: _____   Info: _____

Resource 6: _____

Info: _____   Info: _____

Info: _____   Info: _____

Info: _____   Info: _____

Resource 7: _____

Info: _____   Info: _____

Info: _____   Info: _____

Info: _____   Info: _____

Resource 8: _____

Info: _____   Info: _____

Info: _____   Info: _____

Info: _____   Info: _____

Resource 9: _____

Info: _____   Info: _____

Info: _____   Info: _____

Info: _____   Info: _____

Ancient Music
Worksheets

Ancient Roman Instruments

Mark which instruments you think you hear as you listen to the ancient Roman music of *Synaulia II*.

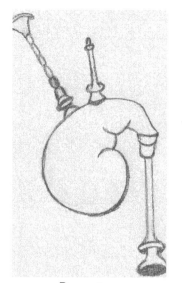

Bagpipe

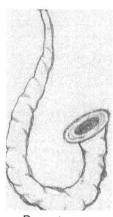

Buccina

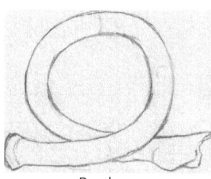

Bugle

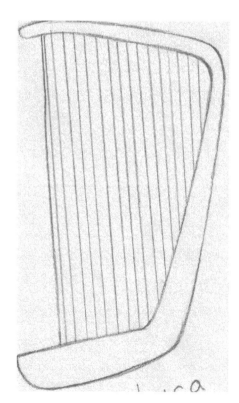

Sambuca

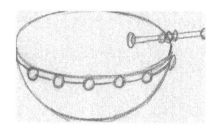

Tympanum

Aulos (wind instrument)

Medieval Instruments

Use this page to draw and write about your medieval instrument.

Instrument name: _____

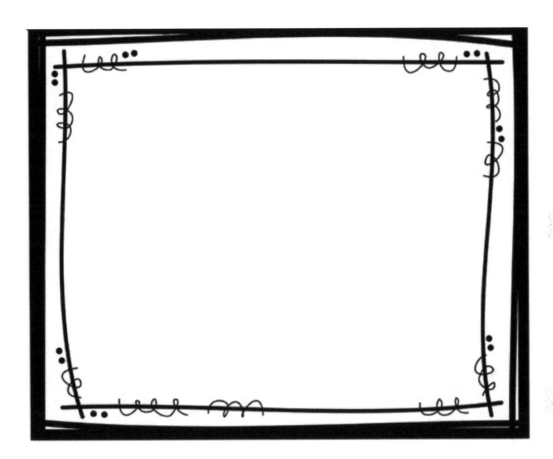

_____

_____

_____

_____

Bible

Worksheets

Compassion

Write on each line someone you should have compassion on

C _____

O _____

M _____

P _____

A _____

S _____

S _____

I _____

O _____

N _____

Creation Circles

Draw or write what God created on the first four days of creation.

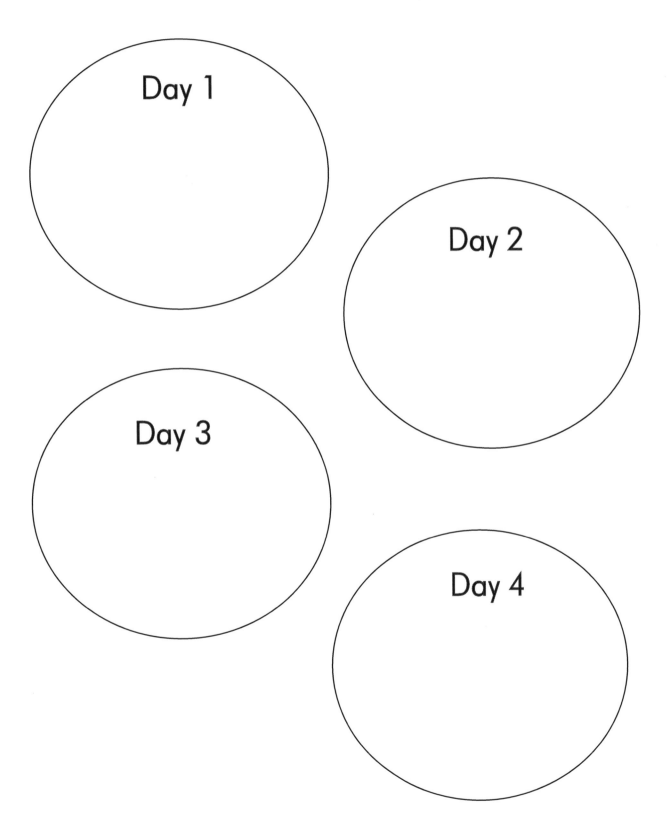

Creation Circles

Draw or write what God created on the last three days of creation. You can color the cover circle if you'd like. Cut out all eight circles and staple them together.

Day 5

Day 6

Day 7

Days of Creation

Ten Commandments

Fill in the Ten Commandments.

1. _____

_____

2. _____

_____

3. _____

_____

4. _____

_____

5. _____

_____

6. _____

_____

7. _____

_____

8. _____

_____

9. _____

_____

10. _____

_____

Made in the USA
Middletown, DE
08 October 2021